Ideas Box!

Light

How did that grow so quickly?

Sarah Ridley

W
FRANKLIN WATTS
LONDON • SYDNEY

espresso
education

First published in 2011

Franklin Watts
338 Euston Road
London NW1 3BH

Franklin Watts Australia
Level 17/207 Kent Street
Sydney, NSW 2000

A CIP catalogue record for this book is available from the British Library.

ISBN: 978 1 4451 0397 6
Dewey: 535

Series Editor: Sarah Peutrill
Art Director: Jonathan Hair
Designer: Matt Lilly
Illustrations: Artful Doodlers

Printed in China

Franklin Watts is a division of Hachette Children's Books, an Hachette UK company. www.hachette.co.uk

Contents

Pages with this symbol have a downloadable photocopiable sheet (see page 30).

Light in the sky

When Sal and Ash went on a school activity week, everyone got up early one morning to watch the Sun rise over the landscape. Feeling cold and tired, they climbed a small hill to get a good view. Back at school, this was one of the favourite parts of the trip that everyone talked about.

Look at the colours!

?

Feedback...

Have you watched a sunrise or a sunset? How would you describe the colours?

The Sun is a huge star, burning in space for billions of years to come. It lights up the eight planets in the solar system, including the Earth. These planets move around, or orbit, the Sun. It takes the Earth a whole year to get round.

Fast facts

- The Sun is 150 million kilometres from Earth.
- Earth is the only planet known to support life.
- The Sun is one of millions of stars out in space.
- All life on Earth depends on light and heat from the Sun.

The Sun is a giant ball of burning gases, sending heat and light out into space.

Quiz:
Which planets lie between Earth and the Sun?

A) Mars and Venus

B) Venus and Mercury

C) Mercury and Mars

Quiz answers are on page 32.

! Never look directly at the Sun. Light from the Sun is very strong and can damage eyesight forever.

Day and night

On Sal and Ash's last evening at the activity centre, everyone gathered around a bonfire. It was very exciting to be out in the dark, with the Moon and the stars. When the fire had died down, the adults led them back to the centre using torches and lanterns.

Can you name the light sources around me?

Sal knows that the Earth spins round once every day. At any one time, half the surface of the Earth is facing the Sun and half is facing away. The part of the Earth that is facing the Sun has daylight while the other half has darkness.

In the night sky, the Moon shines brightly. It does not make any light of its own but reflects light from the Sun. Different amounts of the Moon are lit up by the Sun over the course of a month, so the Moon appears to change shape.

The Moon does not give out its own light so it is not a light source but it reflects the light of the Sun.

History spot: lighting the darkness

In the past, people relied on firelight, candles, oil lamps and rushlights to light their houses. Rushlights could be made at home. Women and children collected and dried out rushes, stripped off almost all of the green outside layer and dipped the rushes in melted animal fat. When lit, the rushlights gave out a weak, yellow light.

A rushlight held in a stand. Rushlights were used from Roman times until about a hundred years ago, especially in poorer homes.

The Sun and seasons

Polly and Eddy enjoy the summer months. They can spend more time outdoors, visit the beach for a day trip or holiday, and enjoy the warmth and longer days.

Why are days longer in summer?

The Earth takes a year to travel around the Sun, and during this time sunlight hits the Earth in different ways. This happens because the Earth is tilted. The part of the Earth that is leaning towards the Sun will have longer days and stronger sunlight, creating spring and then summer. As time passes, the same part of the Earth will be leaning away from the Sun and will have shorter days and weaker sunlight, creating autumn turning to winter.

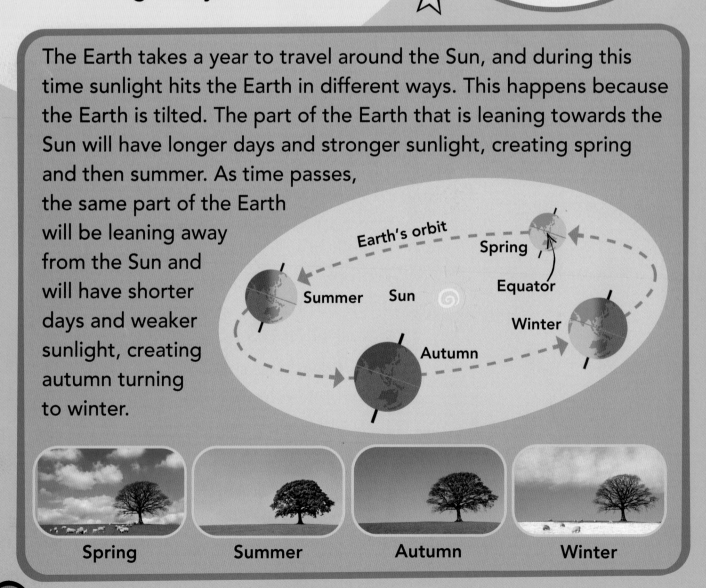

Earth's orbit

Spring

Equator

Summer   Sun

Winter

Autumn

Spring   Summer   Autumn   Winter

Quiz:
The other half of the world has the opposite season. If it is summer in Australia, what season will it be in the United Kingdom?

A) Winter

B) Spring

C) Summer

Ash helped Polly to write an acrostic poem about what she likes about summer. They started each line with a letter from the word 'summer'.

Summer is my favourite time of year,
Under the blue sky I have fun,
Messing about with friends,
Making sandcastles on the beach,
Eating ice cream and summer fruits,
Reading a book under a tree.

Geography spot: days without night

This photo was taken at midnight in Greenland during an Arctic summer.

In the Arctic, the Sun never sets in the summer months. The long days heat up the soil and allow plants to grow and flower in some places. Use an atlas to find Canada, Greenland and other countries that are within the Arctic Circle. Imagine living through an Arctic summer and write a story about it.

Shadow play

Kim, Ash and Eddy enjoy playing in the park. One of Eddy's favourite games is to stand on someone's shadow. The shadow is made because the body blocks the light from the Sun, leaving a person-shaped shadow on the ground.

Shadows change during the day. As the Earth slowly spins around every day, so the Sun's position in the sky changes.

At sunrise, the Sun is low in the sky and shadows are long.

8 o'clock in the morning

History spot: sundials

Before mechanical clocks, people made sundials to tell the time. These varied from simple shadow sticks to complicated sundials with a lot of information on them. Sundials use the fact that shadows change position during the day to mark the passing of time. What time is it by this sundial? Will a sundial work on a cloudy day?

By midday, the Sun is high in the sky and so its light rays hit objects directly, casting little or no shadows.

Midday

In the evening, the Sun is low in the sky and so there are long shadows again.

7 o'clock in the evening

Understanding eclipses

Ash decided to find out about eclipses. An eclipse happens when light from the Sun or Moon is blocked for a short time. During a total solar eclipse, the Moon passes between the Sun and the Earth, blocking sunlight. The sky goes dark and day turns to night for a few minutes. This is because the Earth is lying in the shadow of the Moon.

Ash's mother watched a total solar eclipse in 1999. He interviewed her about the experience.

Ash: How did you know the eclipse was going to occur?
Mum: The newspapers, as well as radio and TV presenters, told us all about it.

Ash: Why was everyone so excited?
Mum: Although total solar eclipses happen around the world every year-and-a-half, it is very rare to see one in the country where you live during your lifetime. There won't be another one here until 2090.

Ash: Did you have to be careful?
Mum: Yes, I had to wear special dark glasses so that I didn't damage my eyes.

Sun

Moon

Earth

Ash: What did it feel like?
Mum: It felt really weird – cold and suddenly dark. Everyone went quiet and the birds fell silent.

Ash: What happened next?
Mum: Slowly the Sun started to reappear and the sky grew light again. I'll always remember it.

Quiz: Why does a solar eclipse occur?

A) The Moon blocks out the light from the Sun.

B) The Earth blocks out the light from the Sun.

C) The planet Mercury blocks out the light from the Sun.

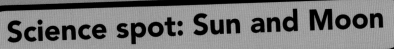

Science spot: Sun and Moon

In the photo of a total solar eclipse (above), the Moon appears to be almost the same size as the Sun as it blocks out the Sun's light. This is not true. In fact, the Sun is about 400 times bigger than the Moon but it is very far away. The Moon blocks sunlight during an eclipse because it is just the right distance away from the Earth.

Light for life

Polly is growing sunflowers. She really enjoys looking after her plants and waters them regularly. After they have flowered, she will leave the seed heads for the birds to feed on during the winter.

Look how tall they have grown!

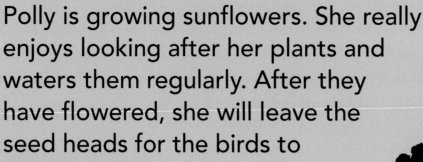

Sunflowers, like all plants, use sunlight to make food. Then animals, including people, eat the plants for food. They may also eat animals that will have eaten plants. In this way, sunlight is vital to all life on Earth.

Farmers grow sunflowers for their seeds. The seeds can be eaten whole or pressed for their oil.

14

A plant's leaves are its food factories. Each leaf has special cells that use sunlight, water and carbon dioxide from air to make plant food. This food travels to all parts of the plant to feed all of its needs.

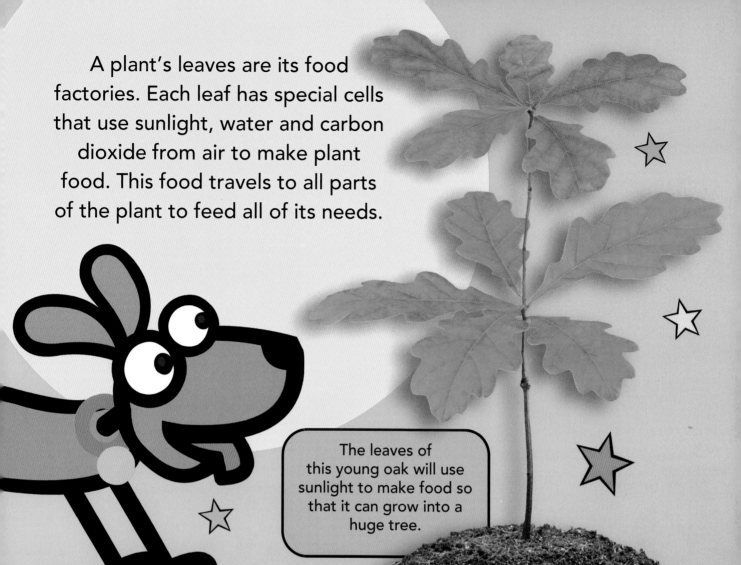

The leaves of this young oak will use sunlight to make food so that it can grow into a huge tree.

PSHE spot: sunlight and health

Sunlight makes people feel happier and healthier. In addition, sunlight helps the skin to make vitamin D. Vitamins are needed for good health but the Sun's light can damage the skin. So try to spend some time outside every day but remember to cover up and wear sun cream if you are outside in the summer between 11 am and 3 pm.

Seeds and shoots

Polly decided to grow some bean seeds in different conditions to see what happens. She grew some in the light, and others in the dark. She predicted that the ones in the dark would not grow well as she knows that plants need light to grow. Grow your own to see what happens.

You will need:

- 4 plastic cups
- 4 bean seeds
- Soil or compost
- Water
- Black paper
- Sticky tape
- Scissors

1 Fill each cup with soil or compost.

2 Push a bean down into each cup and give them all a little water.

3 Place two of the cups on a sunny windowsill.

4 Make two paper cones for the other cups. Cut out a circle of black paper, cut it in half and use sticky tape to form each into a cone.

5 Place two of the filled cups in a dark cupboard and add their cone 'hats' on top, to help prevent any light reaching the seed.

6 Water all the pots equally, every two or three days.

What will happen next?

Polly cared for her seeds and checked them for any changes. Between three to seven days later, the bean seeds in the sunlight pushed up a shoot. Over the next few days, the shoots formed leaves. The ones in the cupboard took longer to sprout. They produced weak, pale shoots as there was enough food in the seed to do this. However, without light, they did not grow strongly.

Fast facts
- Plants need sunlight.
- Plants need water.
- Plants need warmth.

?

Feedback...

Do you like growing plants?
Which plants have you grown?

Rainbows

It had been raining all afternoon. Ash and Scully decided to go out in the garden anyway, as the rain had almost stopped. As soon as they opened the back door they saw a rainbow.

When a rainbow forms, the band of red is always at the top, with the other colours following in a pattern.

A rainbow happens when sunlight passes through raindrops, splitting the light into seven different colours. These are red, orange, yellow, green, blue, indigo and violet. White sunlight is a mixture of these colours. To find a rainbow on a bright showery day you need to have the Sun behind you, as the rainbow forms opposite the Sun.

Try this on a sunny day. Spray water from a garden hose into the air, keeping the Sun behind you. You should see light split into the colours of the rainbow.

Rainbows can also form in the mist of water droplets hanging over a waterfall.

English spot: mnemonics

Use this rhyme to remember the order of the colours in a rainbow. **R**ichard **o**f **Y**ork **g**ave **b**attle **i**n **v**ain. **R**ed, **o**range, **y**ellow, **g**reen, **b**lue, **i**ndigo (a dark shade of purple) and **v**iolet. Rhymes can be useful to help remember facts. They have a special name – a mnemonic (say 'nemonic'). Make them up yourself or memorise famous ones to stun your friends.

?

Feedback...

Have you seen a rainbow? Where were you and what were you doing at the time?

Make a rainbow spinner

Polly and Eddy made a rainbow spinner to see how rainbow colours can be made to join together into white light. Follow their instructions to make one of your own.

You will need:

- White cardboard
- Colour felt-tips or pencils
- Cup or glass
- Ruler
- 120 centimetres of string
- Scissors
- Maths compass

1 Draw around a cup to make a circle on the cardboard. Cut it out carefully.

2 Divide the circle into six equal sections by drawing a line down the middle, top to bottom and then draw an 'X'. Repeat on the other side.

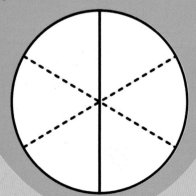

3 Starting with red, colour in each section in the order that they appear in a rainbow. Red, orange, yellow, green, blue, purple (on this spinner, you will mix indigo/violet). Don't forget to colour in the other side.

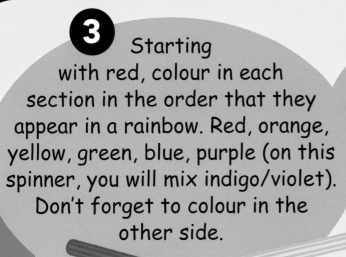

4 Use the compass to make two small holes near the centre of the circle.

5 Thread the string through one hole and back through the other one and join the ends together with a knot.

Why can't I see the colours any more?

6 Pull the string through the holes so that there is an equal amount on each side of the spinner. Twist the spinner and then let it go.

The colours are moving so fast that your eyes see them as white.

Painting light

Sal's hobby is painting and drawing. She finds that her pictures turn out best if she works by the window or outside. Natural light helps her to see colours as they really are.

When Sal wants to show shadows in her pictures, she works carefully. She has to notice where the light is coming from so that the shadows are in the right place.

On a sunny day, the colours are brighter all around. If Sal wants her picture to be full of light, she uses bright colours and lots of white. If she paints the same scene in the evening, the colours are less bright and the sky more grey. For a night scene, she uses darker colours, or adds black to colours to make them darker.

Art spot: shades of blue

Sal decided to have some fun with the colour blue.
She cut a long strip of paper and then marked out
blocks. She squeezed blue liquid paint into two
small containers and used some of it to paint the
middle section. Then, block by block, she added a
little white paint to one of the blue paints and
painted it on, and a little black to the other.
Each block is a paler or darker shade
of the first blue.

Joseph Mallord William Turner (1775–1851)
became known as the 'painter of light'. Here is
one of his paintings, *The Fighting Temeraire*.

Turn the light on!

When Kim woke up suddenly in the night he turned on his light to see the time. The next morning, Kim decided to find out who invented the light bulb and wrote this piece for the school newspaper.

Espresso Extra

Our reporter, Kim, investigates who invented the light bulb.

SWAN VERSUS EDISON

In 1879, Joseph Swan of England and Thomas Edison of the United States of America both claimed to have invented the light bulb. But which one was right?

The invention itself

Both men had successfully invented a glass bulb with a carbon filament, a thin wire, inside that gave out light when electricity passed into it.

Swan

Twenty years earlier, Swan invented a light bulb with a filament made of platinum, a very expensive metal. For years he tried to find a cheaper material that would work as well and eventually succeeded with one made of carbon.

This light bulb was invented by Swan and Edison.

Edison

Edison tried out a lot of materials for a light bulb filament. He also discovered that carbon worked best and announced that he had invented the light bulb in 1879.

What happened next?

At first Edison sent lawyers to argue that he was the true inventor of the light bulb. In the end he agreed to share the invention with Swan. They set up a company to make light bulbs.

Maths spot: count the light bulbs

People rely on light bulbs to carry on their lives once darkness falls. Take a notepad and walk around your house counting up how many light bulbs there are in each room. How will you collect the data? You could compare how many light bulbs there are in different rooms of the house and display the information on a graph.

City lights dazzle the eye and allow everyone to carry on their lives, despite the dark.

⚠ Remember to turn off lights, TV and video game players and phone chargers when you leave a room to save electricity.

How do we see?

Kim, Ash and Polly went to the theatre together. Just before the show started, all the lights went down and they sat in darkness. Then the lights went up and the show began.

Rays of light from the theatre lights beamed down onto the stage and then bounced off the actors and objects on the stage, to enter the children's eyes. There the rays of light hit the back of the eyes where information travels to the brain. The brain made sense of the information and told them what they were seeing.

People cannot see well in the dark but some animals can. Nocturnal animals sleep by day and move around to feed and be active at night. They often have huge round eyes, to draw in what little light there is from starlight or moonlight. They don't expect to see everything clearly and have developed excellent senses of hearing and touch.

The bush baby is a nocturnal animal with great hearing and huge eyes to see in the dark.

Science spot: flashing animals

Some animals can create flashes of light. Female fireflies (below) mix chemicals inside their bodies to make a bright light used to attract a male. Some fish that live in the deepest, darkest waters use flashes of light to attract and confuse their prey.

Female fireflies light up this bush.

Holy light

In Sal's class, the pupils share what they know about different world religions. They notice that light is important in many faiths. Light is often linked to good or God and dark to evil or bad events. Many religions have festivals that involve light.

Sal worked with some of her classmates to write reports about two festivals of lights, Diwali and Hanukkah.

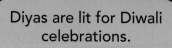

Diyas are lit for Diwali celebrations.

Diwali

(October or November)
This is the Hindu festival of lights, also celebrated by Sikhs. People decorate homes, temples and other buildings with strings of electric lights and small lamps called diyas. The lights welcome the goddess of wealth, Lakshmi, and keep away evil. Children receive gifts and everyone enjoys firework displays and special foods.

Hanukkah (November or December)

Jewish people celebrate their festival of lights at Hanukkah. The festival remembers the miracle that occurred 2,000 years ago in the Temple in Jerusulem. An oil lamp, used in a ceremony to make the Temple holy again after it had been damaged, lasted eight days instead of one. Jewish people celebrate Hanukkah by lighting candles on a special candlestick called a menorah, giving gifts and eating special meals.

> Each evening during Hanukkah, one more candle is lit on a menorah. The ninth candle on the menorah is used to light the others.

History spot: the eternal flame

Light as a flame can be used to remember those who have died. Under the Arc de Triomphe in Paris, France, an eternal flame burns on the Tomb of the Unknown Soldier. It is in memory of soldiers who died during the world wars but were never identified. Find out about other eternal flames around the world.

Glossary

Arc de Triomphe Huge stone arch in Paris, France, started by Napoleon I in 1806.

Arctic The area of land and sea around the North Pole.

Arctic Circle The line drawn on maps and globes to show the areas north of the line where the Sun does not rise at midwinter, or set at midsummer.

carbon The light strong material used to make the filament in a light bulb.

carbon dioxide A gas found in the air.

cell The tiny building block from which all living things are made.

eclipse During an eclipse, light from the Sun or Moon is blocked for a short while.

eternal Never ending.

filament The thin thread of material inside a light bulb.

light source Something that gives out light, including the Sun, fires, candles, electric lights, torches and lighthouses.

natural light Used to describe daylight from the Sun, rather than electric light, candle light or firelight.

nocturnal Animals that are more active at night than in the daytime.

prey Animal hunted and killed as food for another animal.

ray A line of light.

reflect When rays of light (or heat) bounce off an object.

rush A tall, slim plant that grows in damp areas and by rivers and ponds.

senses People have five senses – sight, hearing, touch, taste and smell.

shadow clock A simple sundial using a stick and marks on the ground.

solar system The eight planets, asteroids and comets that orbit the Sun.

sun damage Too much sunlight can make the skin age and can lead to skin cancer.

sundial A clock that uses the position of the Sun in the sky, and the shadows it casts, to tell the time.

Richard of York (1452–1485) Richard was King of England between 1483 and 1485.

temple A place of worship in several religions.

vitamin D One of several vitamins needed for good health. It helps build strong bones and teeth and protects against several diseases.

Activity sheets

Go to www.franklinwatts.co.uk/downloads for free activity sheets.
Page 11: A template and instructions to make a simple sundial.
Page 19: A page of useful rhymes to aid memory.
Page 28: Instructions to make a diya lamp.

Espresso connections

Here are a few ideas for how to take the contents of this book further using Espresso.

Light in the sky (pages 4–5)
Science 2 > Earth, Moon and Sun has videos and fact files and quizzes about the solar system.

Day and night (pages 6–7)
Visit *Science 2 > Earth, Moon and Sun*, for videos, a quiz and a learning pathway about day and night. *Science 1 > Light and Dark* has material on light sources. For more information about fireworks and bonfires, use the *Firework night* collections in *History 1* and *2*. *History 2* also has a module on life in Tudor times.

The Sun and seasons (pages 8–9)
Science 2 > Earth, Moon and Sun has videos and learning resources about the seasons, as well as information about the weather at the Poles. Go to *Maths 2 > Maths activities* Resource Box > *Handling data* about weather and seasons. *Geography 2 > News archive* has many stories about seasonal and unseasonal weather.

Shadow play (pages 10–11)
There are resources about shadows in *Science 2 > Light and shadows*, including information about sundials in *Further resources*.

Understanding eclipses (pages 12–13)
Eclipses are covered in *Science 2 > Light and shadows* and *Science 2 > Earth, Moon and Sun*.

Light for life (pages 14–15)
New Life Resource box in *Science 1* and *Harvest and food* Resource box in *Science 2* support the content of this spread. For a video storybook about sunflowers, go to *English 1 > Big Books > Camille and the Sunflowers* by Lawrence Anholt. The *News archives* in *PSHE 1* and *2* have news articles on staying safe in the Sun.

Seeds and shoots (pages 16–17)
For related resources, look in *Growing plants* in *Science 1*. There are several pieces encouraging children to grow plants or take up gardening in the *Science 2 > News archive > Plants*.

Rainbows/Make a rainbow spinner (pages 18–21)
English 2 > Poetry Workshop has many ideas for writing poems or rhymes.

Painting light (pages 22–23)
Art 2 > A sense of place > Techniques explores colour and tone. The Impressionists section of the *Artists collection* in *Art 2* focuses on how the artists depicted light in their paintings.

Turn the light on! (pages 24–25)
Science 2 > Electricity has videos on the history of electricity and on the invention of the light bulb including a cartoon history of the competition between Swan and Edison. For news articles relating to saving energy and green energy, go to the *News archive* and *Sustainability* in *Geography 2*. *English 2 > Newspapers* and *News* Resource box gives ideas on how to write newspaper articles.

How do we see? (pages 26–27)
For videos and fact files on the eye and seeing, go to *Science 2 > Light and Shadows > How we see*.

Holy light (pages 28–29)
In *RE 2* the Diwali collection includes videos and instructions to make a diya lamp. There is also a Hanukkah Collection in *RE 1* and *2*. The *News* archive in *RE 1* has videos about festivals of light worldwide. *History 2 > News archive > First World War* has several videos about Remembrance Sunday.

Index

Quiz answers
Page 5: B) Venus and Mercury
Page 9: A) Winter
Page 13: A) The Moon blocks out
the light from the Sun.

These are the lists of contents for each title in *Espresso Ideas Box!*:

Chocolate
Where does chocolate come from? • How do cacao trees grow? • Cacao farming • The history of chocolate • Make a collage of the Aztec chocolate god • The chocolate trade • Make a chocolate piñata • Manufacturing chocolate • Is chocolate good for me? • Melting chocolate • Make chocolate leaves • Chocolate recipes • Chocolate heaven • Glossary and Activity sheets • Espresso connections

Light
Light in the sky • Day and night • The Sun and seasons • Shadow play • Understanding eclipses • Light for life • Seeds and shoots • Rainbows • Make a rainbow spinner • Painting light • Turn the light on! • How do we see? • Holy light • Glossary and Activity sheets • Espresso connections

Rainforests
What is a rainforest? • Rainforests around the world • Rainforest river • Life on the forest floor • Up in the trees • Play the music of the rainforest • Colourful rainforests • Animals in danger • Make a rainforest game • People of the rainorest • Disappearing rainforests • Save the rainforest • Have a rainforest debate • Glossary and Activity sheets • Espresso connections

The Olympics
The Olympic Games • The ancient Olympics • Events at the ancient Olympics • The modern Olympics • Design an Olympic kit • All about the events • Track and field • The Winter Olympics • The Paralympics • Games around the world • What makes an Olympic champion? • Medals and world records • Make an Olympics board game • Glossary and Activity sheets • Espresso connections • Index and quiz answers

Water
Water! • Solid, liquid, gas • The water cycle • Snow, hail and rain • Rivers • Floods • Painting water • Drinking water • Down the drain • Water and plants • Sacred water • Powerful water • Water for fun • Glossary and Activity sheets • Espresso connections

Where you live
What is special about where you live? • Finding out about the past • What is the natural history of your area? • The square metre project • What can maps tell us? • Make a map stick • Changes to your area • Who lives in your area? • What jobs do people do? • Make a picture quiz • What problems are there in your area? • Famous connections • Attracting visitors to your area • Glossary and Activity sheets • Espresso connections